The E

coaster

Maynna Pandey

About the book

This book is all about a girl named Trinetra Ahuja, a young teen of 17 who's often stuck in the whirlpool of her thoughts and yet manages to tell her story.

Note : The characters in the story may or may not exist in the reality but the

instances mentioned definitely can be representing someone's life. This is not to offend any mindset or any sort of beliefs. It's a story and should be read as a story only. It's about a young girl , Trinetra who's having a major difference of thoughts and narrates her tale of transition from 2020 to 2022(until now) . It's now upon the reader to judge whether transitions moulded her strong or puzzled her in the emotions or both. Also, the word “I" is majorly used by Trinetra herself and it's not the author out there. But, more than 10 small paragraphs are the feelings of the Author itself.

Table of Contents

1. Brief Introduction

2. Insights regarding education

& personal life

3. New responsibilities and learnings

4. Puzzled in her thoughts

5. Her edgy & risky behaviour

6. Extents of a teenager's behaviour

7. Some secrets and grudges

8. Author's take on her

9. 2020-22 Phase of universal transitions

LET'S BEGIN!!!

Hey all,

My name is Trinetra Kailash Ahuja and I am 17 years old. I study in Grade 11 (Humanities) at Brixtonne International School, Ludhiana. I live with my father (Kailash) , mother (Nakshatra) and my younger sibling (Hriday). I love to compose songs and to write poems. My father works as a senior pilot for Lufthansa Airways and my mother is a clinical psychologist. While my brother is in class 7th at Laurasia International School.

So, that was a short insight about me and

my family. Now, let's dig deep into my life. I am in love with studies but not a great fan of sports except badminton. I am a decent scorer with 83% in Class 10th Boards. English and Hindi are my favourites whereas science and maths threatened me for years.

From class 6th, I started falling in the subjects I hate. I remember I just entered class 10th with 30/80 in Maths and 57 in Science. The reason I think is that I am an emotional person rather than a logical one. I feel an enhanced connection with English and Hindi. In class 8th, I met another hurdle named Sanskrit. I feel that still my mind is of a grade 8th kid because that was the last physical school before the Great Lockdown.

Great Lockdown lasted more than a year and came into our lives due to COVID-19. The city of Wuhan, China is considered to be the birthplace of this pandemic. That was the first time adults worked from home and kids studied online. This had never happened even with our grandparents. But new generations come up with new changes. In 2020, I was in Class 9th and Hriday was in 5th in the same school. The experience of online studies fascinated me initially but later on felt like a prison. Although our parents and the school gave us the best facilities still studying in the school environment along with friends was far better. My parents planned me to gift a phone in Class 11th but the pandemic forced them to drop the plan. My father suggested me to buy a new one but my mother insisted my father to buy a new phone for him and give me his older phone. I was also with mom's notion. So, I got my first phone in July 2020 and was set to make new projects and to complete other school activities. But, as all of us know, a teen's mind is full of fluctuations. I started spending my maximum leisure time on the phone and one night a scolding changed everything.

Due to zero physical activities, I started gaining weight crazily. I have been bubbly since birth. At that time my weight was 78 kgs. I was just

14 at that time. There were frequent comparisons between me in the older photos and me in the current time which made me extremely negative.

Along with weight problems, I had hot feuds with my parents. They often talked upon my weight only.

I know that they don't wanted any problems for me but

even just a word upon my physique made me sad. So, my father came up with a new approach which was scientific. Although it was for 18+ people but I really needed it.

The stipulated meal system: It Just organized my eating and exercising habits. 30 minutes to eat and 45 minutes to walk at night. I gave into it from 6th

Jan 2021 and I am happy with the results. I slashed out 12 to 13 kilos without any major diet changes. Now, I just eat 3 big meals and a snack meal. But, I miss my long hairs of 2020. I never had big hairs and when I had, I didn't maintained it. “A person can never be perfect” and the same was with me. Either physique or hairfall, I was always in between them.

From the saying, I remembered my first gynaecologist visit. I started menstruating before 9 days of my 13th birthday and they were never regular. I often missed them. My insane plump physique contributed more in the irregularities. I didn't wanted to have this visit but was forced to do so. One so-called fine day, my parents took me to Keya Women Care. My doctor's name was Keya Rajpurohit. She was an old and experienced doctor. She asked my age and was happy to

know that I write

poems (The ability to

write is a blessing

and I was blessed

with it on 13th Feb

2020) . She checked

my blood pressure

and it was damn

high. She carried on with the check up and suggested a **diabetes** and a **thyroid** test.

I was very furious on my parents. None of my friends have

gone to such doctors. But, my fate had another plans. The doctor made my mother understand that it will get regular from her 16th year and if not, she will perform a sonography upon me. The fact that shocked me was that my father knew that I was menstruating. Luckily, I neither had **thyroid** nor **diabetes**.

My parents don't ask much about my cramps or pains. Also, I don't throw any chocolatey tantrums that are much famous in western countries. By the way, I love western culture and

songs.

Shawn Mendes &
Alec

Benjamin are my favourites.

Although, lockdown

created many

differences between

me and my parents

in particular yet they

love me a lot and I

love them.

2020, just made me

feel lonely and being

imprisoned in one's

own house. Hoping **2021** will be better than this but I was wrong. Schools were partially open and I went to my school for final exams with **masks** on and **hand sanitizer** within reach along with 6ft distance from others. But, again COVID-19 brought another wave that was immensely dangerous. April was the worst of all. Firstly, my **father's**

elder brother died due to the **pandemic** and then my **maternal grandmother**; after fighting a **long battle** against **paralysis** for 10 years gave up. It was frightening to lose 2 members of extended family within a week.

Later on, kids of my age were vaccinated. We were allowed to attend full-time schools and I finally breathed in fresh air regularly. Also, relations were getting better by the passing phase.

I gave my Class 10th Boards in a unique manner. They were conducted in 2 terms and I proudly passed in both of them. Though maths was becoming tough to crack but after failing in pre-boards 2 with just 11/40 in Maths, I realised that I needed help. My father taught me the chapters and I scored what everyone expected from me.

Again in the hope of **2022** being a better year, I celebrated on

31st December. The first 3 months were full of exams for me. Basically, It was hectic but poems boosted my will.

Suddenly, my mom started feeling

fatigued. She was restless and was **losing weight**. She never told anyone in the family. Maybe because me and my brother were having exams and also my father was busy during the month. But her power to **tolerate** was over in **March.**

After **pre board 2,** my mother wanted herself to get checked. She also went to MS. Keya only. After coming home, she pretended to be fine and good. But it wasn't the case. Visits to hospital increased during my board exams. She even had an operation. We continuously asked what was the case, but they were hesitant to inform.

I **stocked** them. I went through mum's

internet history and found a lead. Later, I checked her files and reports secretly. I was devastated. I remember crying more than 10 times. But I wanted to be strong for my parents. My parents had frequent **Mumbai** visits and relatives started coming over to look after us. During that time, I learned to manage the house and the adults supported me too. I remember my parents were in Mumbai and my maternal uncle missed his flight to Ludhiana. That was the most creepy and scary night. I literally couldn't sleep.

Once, I overheard my parents saying about **discontinuing our education** and one night, they were discussing a major report of mum by closing the room's door and after that tour to Mumbai started if in case they couldn't stay with us. They managed well and thankfully I am in

11th right now.

They returned from

Mumbai in May after

the 1st operation. I

saw my mother in

somewhat in

comfort about

knowing what's wrong with her but highly uncomfortable due to the operation. Her first few words just made me immensely emotional – **"Kaisi hai meri beti"**

(How's my daughter). She usually used my nickname to refer me. But after such a long time, she used the word **“beti"** or **“daughter”**. I had a flood of tears in my eyes due to which I couldn't turn back and reply. I wasn't happy. I felt **worthless** and **incapable** due to my **minor age.**

Afterwards, the treatment started in Ludhiana itself.

Whenever my father went out on a trip, a strange fear always haunted me. Even now, I couldn't sleep unless I hear his voice. But now I had the same feelings for my mother. Actually, a few years back, a friend of mine also saw her mother suffering from the same disease. So, I wanted to dedicate a **poem** to my friend and her mother. I consider myself as the **guilty** for my mom suffering from the same. This made my bond even more stronger.

Still, my mum's in the post-op recovery and treatment. It's a long process and very expensive too. Such incidents teaches an individual the value of **self-health** &

money. For privacy, I couldn't name the disease but it's a chronic one.

Whenever I managed the house, I felt as the **crude woman of the household.** Here,

I am recording it via writing it.

3 SECRETS OF MINE WHICH MY PARENTS DON'T KNOW :

At 10, I stole the money and spent it

on chips and
chocolates for 10
days with my
younger brother.

I didn't revealed
that I knew
about the

disease because

of stocking.

I often cry at night

due to past

flashbacks.

During all these

times, my **father** has

been the most **balanced** one. He never made us feel lack of anything. He has always been a perfect husband and an excellent father. He is always the one

I look upto for the balance.

Even my **mother** has been a **badass woman**. She is the strongest person I have ever seen. I really can't live without my family.

No matter how big are the differences, we always get back together..

One night, I was having a normal sleep and I didn't had anything negative in my mind. Suddenly, near 5 am next morning; I had **tears** in my eyes. I was experiencing **shortness of breath.** I couldn't even utter a word to call someone. I had a nightmare in which I was being told that I am **losing** my mother. Literally, I was believing in it. I started fighting with everyone. My body was full of sweat. After all this, I afraid of sleeping for 2 days. Still that memory haunts me bad.

So talking about now;

I am still making new friends at school. My new school is a

heaven. While, My Lil bro is entering into TEENAGE and is having a hard time with teachers especially.

Recently Diwali was on the door and I was almost set to

welcome it but after **Dhanteras**, I was hosted by my **Menses.** The worst thing, a girl could experience. I cried for 2 reasons:

1. Yup, I got my October cycle

2. Shit, I cannot participate in anything religious.

Due to all this, I couldn't help my mum lighting **diyas** or making **Rangolis**.

The first 2 days were worst. My family was enjoying **Ind-Pak match** and my lower back was hitting me like anything. Cramps in stomach made difficult for me to sit. I was compensating and distracting myself from ice cream. Later on, things got on track.

But I promise myself that I'll do something big and will definitely learn to control my emotions to succeed. I love my family and I am grateful to have them. I won't let differences in my relations growing any bigger. I won't stop smiling. No matter how black or dark conditions get, I will stand strong and vibrant like yellow colour.

See, Trinetra is someone who knows who and what is

good for her, but her emotions puzzle her bad. However, she is constantly determined to improve and no matter how many times her beliefs are broken, she won't stop hoping to improve and get better. Now I know why is it important to channelize yourself especially during TEENAGE. Sometimes, her parents are someone she needs.

Sometimes, parents vs her.

As you know, she isn't good at cooking and their was rough conflict between her and the mother. She was furious because she is egoistic. She went to her bed and started crying. When tears couldn't resolve her pain, she tried to harm herself. She started punching in the walls and this lasted for an hour.

She was like : I should move ahead the bed, grab a scarf and make away with herself.

But she controlled
herself. She keeps
having negative
thoughts about her.
Her current favourite
is self-harm.

She keeps missing
the physical touches

like hugs or head pats from her father. Once she got hurt from a steel chair during studying and when her father patted and rolled his hand over her hairs, she was elated. She forgot her pain. From there on, she thought that her discomfort will bring in more attention.

Her father does the same to her brother Hriday no matter

what is the situation. She literally falls for it. She wants people around her to realize such things. I guess you all consider her as **MS. Tantrum thrower.**

But that's not what

I ponder about her.

As per my view, she

yearns for love. She

cannot tolerate

anger of her loved

ones. She clearly is

less expensive and

an introvert maybe

suffering from **lower selective mutism. She hesitates to speak out her heart. She avoids eye contact. Her inhibitions stop her a lot.**

This concept must be new for all.

It is a complex Childhood and Teenage anxiety disorder which is responsible for an individual's lower **SOCIAL quotient.** It shouldn't be left untreated.

See, inhibitions, anxiety and a person's behaviour are all different. Anxiety is not only a **bread earner** suffers from. It can happen to anyone and anytime.

However, she isn't weak at focusing. She studies hard. It's just that she lives in her comfort zone only. She wishes to do something big and she is purely capable for it.

Look, her parents are not hitlers. They support her at every step. They try to advance themselves as per the time but however earlier these 4 had different **thoughts.** Now they cannot **connect** with each other which is not correct. These severed connections later lead to isolation in relationships.

Sometimes, being together with loved ones isn't enough. Relationships should have lesser judgements and

Trinetra thinks her family is judgy at times. She even stopped revealing her weight to anyone.

The last 3 years (2020,2021 & 2022 is

gonna end soon) has been on tough on Trinetra and many other young kids & teenagers especially. Most of them are stuck in between of their **thoughts** & the **reality**. This story must have been the story of someone reading her tale right now.

Not a single story is good or bad. It all depends upon the reader's perspective.

As an observer, this tale has been full of values and emotions for me. I hope the one reading this derives out the feelings of oneness between Trinetra and him/Her especially over emotional feelings and learns to control those. I advice everyone not to go crazy like Trinetra or call her insane.

Maybe these years

have been average

for her but it may be

the best for

someone else.

Just Remember :

Whether the time

is good or bad, it

will pass out quickly.

I am sure Trinetra must be startled to read it. To know, how risky or edgy she is. She is not just a character but a human representing herself and the

thought of her

reading my book is

crazy enough 😅🙄.

Let you be the

master of your

emotions and

not the opposite

should be the

truth.

A note from the Author

I am elated to complete my 1st short story book and to put forward a brand new human perspective. I hope the language used in the story was easy to catch and you read it without being a complete judgemental.

The instances of the story may be a truth to somebody and I am happy if I could connect with my readers. I wish everyone the best wishes and just never give up. Be unique and come out in the world. There's no one to stop you. It's very important to channelize your

energies and

emotions.

CPSIA information can be obtained
at www.ICGtesting.com
Printed in the USA
LVHW030753251122
733912LV00005B/132

9 789356 754140